Savoury Reminiscence

By

Seemab Zahra

"To teach is to learn."

— Imam Ali

Du'a Kumail

Introduction

In Pakistan special emphasis is given to teaching girls how to cook, but my case was different. My parents stressed the importance of education rather than teaching me how to cook. My mother cooked, and we all enjoyed her delicacies. However, when I was getting married, and moving to Canada, my mother thought of a plan and wrote down all her recipes on papers and gave them to me to take along. These recipes included very simple recipes such as making Daal (lentil soup) and boiling rice, to some very complex ones like Kofta curry masala (meatball curry) and Kababs. I kept those recipes in my suitcase like sacred manuscripts and followed them like commandments.

I still have those recipes. They helped me a lot in the beginning, but gradually, I learned new recipes from various cultures and my mother-in-law who was born in Lucknow, India. She taught me many Indian recipes.

Now that I have recipes from my mother and my mother-in-law, I want to pass them on to my daughters, so they can cook and enjoy authentic Pakistani and Indian food when they grow up.

Table of Contents

Table of Contents

Acknowledgments

When I submitted my proposal for Micro-grant for Waterloo Region Artists 2020 by Pat the Dog Theatre Creation, I had no idea that this tiny idea in my mind will ultimately become a published recipe book. It started with a proposal for a photography project with the intention to capture food from various cultures in Waterloo Region, but the pandemic changed everything. With back-to-back lockdowns, I could not start my work on the project until August 2021, and then my plan changed once again. What commenced with the idea of archiving food belonging to diverse cultures, ended with documenting my very own best recipes.

This book was made possible with the generous grant by Pat the Dog Theatre Creation. I am thankful to PTD for giving me the opportunity and awarding me with Micro-grant for Waterloo Region Artists 2020 and 2021.

I am also grateful to this land where I come as a guest, a land which is the ancestral home of Anishinaabe, Haudenosaunee, and Neutral People. As a settler, I thank the Indigenous people for allowing me to live here and benefit from its resources.

In addition to the generous grant by PTD, I must thank a lot of people who gave me the courage to make this happen. First of all, thanks to my husband and daughters for bearing with me and supporting me through the process.

Thanks to Pam Patel from MT Space for acknowledging my potential and providing me with a platform to showcase my creative skills, Carolina Miranda for inspiring me through Feminine Harbor, mentoring me, and later taking me on board. Thank you for taking me into that spiritual domain where I could understand what it means to be a Matriarch. Thank you for helping me understand the importance of this land and how it recognizes its daughters and embraces them.

I would also like to thank several Arts companies and theatres in the Waterloo Region who believed in me when I doubted myself. Thank you KW Poetry Slam, Textile Magazine, Green Lights Arts Theatre, MT Space, Women's Room at the University of Waterloo, The Community Edition, Coalition of Muslim Women of KW, MuseArts Toronto, THEMUSEUM Kitchener, London Regional Social Forum, Crossing Borders, Martin Luther University College at Wilfrid Laurier University, Strong Start to Reading, Feminine Harbor, The Article Club, The Remnant Archive (India), HumSub.com, The Friday Times, NayaDaur from Pakistan, Arts Awards Waterloo Region, CAFKA, and Conrad Grebel University College at the University of Waterloo. All these organizations have helped me grow and gather the courage to continue to write and believe in what I write.

A big thanks to Lisa O'Connell, Bashar Lulu Jabour, Janice Jo Lee, Ryan Antooa, Andy Myles, Fitsum Areguy, my mentors: Dr. Naweed Syed (Calgary), Uncle Hashmat Abbas (Toronto), Fauzia Mazhar from CMW-KW, Farnood Alam, and Husnain Jamal (Pakistan), Mr. Iqbal Haider (Calgary), Dr. Umer Farooq, Dr. M. Pasha Khan, Dr. Naveed Iftikhar, Dr. Sajid Raheem, Paola Gomez, my friends: Nazrana Yousufzai, Maqsood Asi, Muhammad Shoaib, Minhaj, Dr. Hina, Nadia, and my childhood friends for your endless support and kindness.

Thanks to sister Hend Hegazi for helping with editing, Laila El Mugammar for introducing me to the magic of self-designing, and self-publishing and for supporting me through the process.

I am also grateful to the very talented Zehra Nawab whose extraordinary, beautiful illustrations inspired me in many ways. Thank you for designing this Book's cover and illustrating my very first creative rendition in such beautiful colors.

A little thanks to myself for mustering up the courage to break the shackles of silence and to Abbu and Ammi without whom I would have never been able to move even a stick. If only every girl in this world had parents like mine, this world would be a better place.

Alhumdulillah!

I dedicate this book
To all the women from whom I am
And all the women who are from me;
Amma (my maternal grandmother
whom I lost to COVID-19),
My paternal grandmother
whom I could never meet,
My mother
who is my strength,
My mother-in-law
who taught me so much,
And my daughters
Meriam, Masooma, and Fatema
who inspired me to write this book.

Behold the recipes, and memories.

Churi Kay Laddu

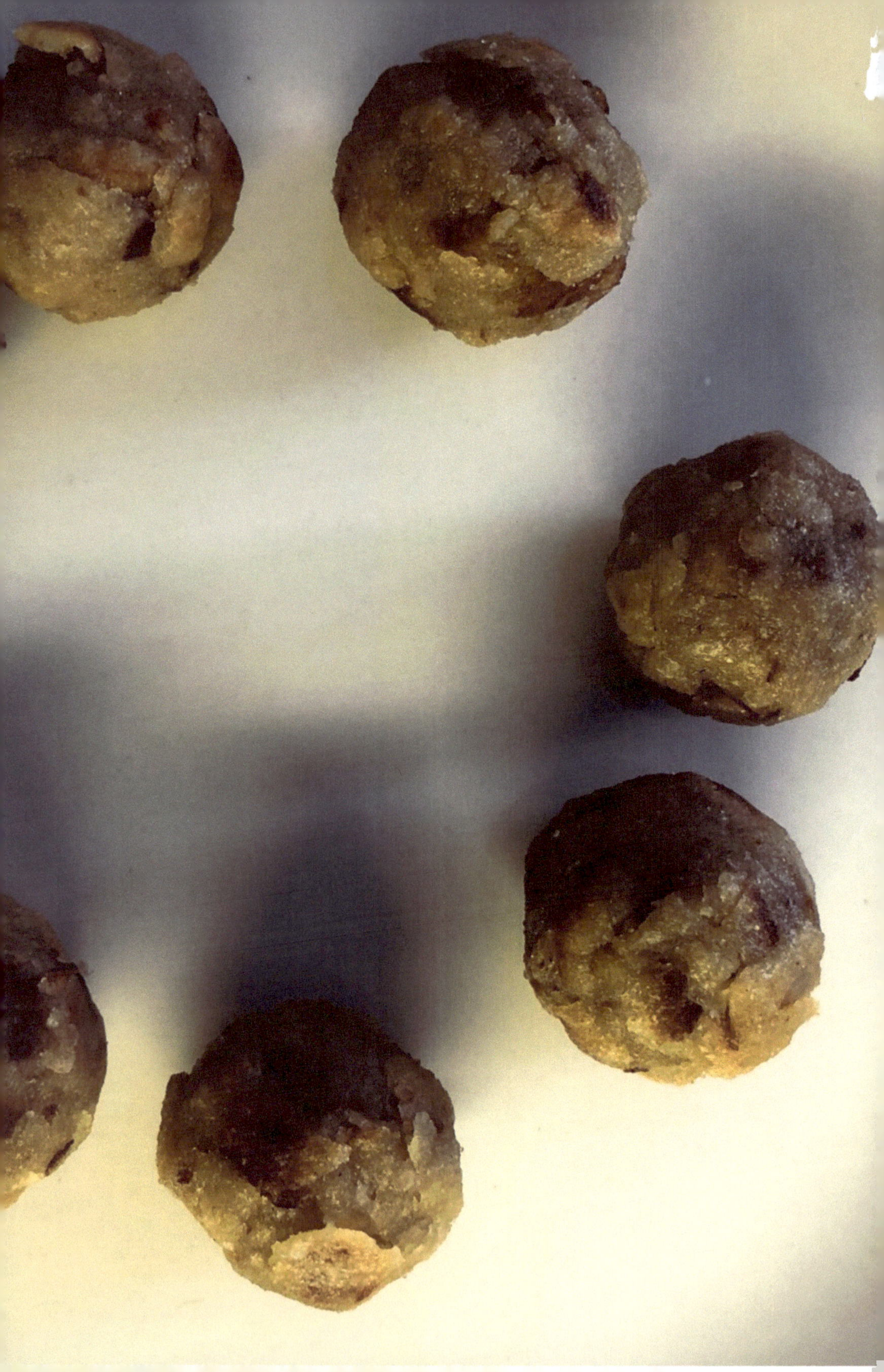

I lost my maternal grandmother (Nani) during the COVID-19 pandemic. She was in her eighties. If one word could define my Nani, it would be "Queen." Queen, because she never had to worry about any of the domestic chores. My grandfather was an agriculturist and a farmer, so they always had a lot of domestic help. Though my Nani almost never cooked, there was one thing that she used to make for her grandchildren, and that was Churi kay Laddu. Churi means crumbs, and Laddu means small sweet edible spheres.

She would ask Buwa (her cook) to make a Paratha (Flatbread made with oil mixed inside the dough) and bring it to her while it was still hot. She would break it into small pieces, and quickly mix sugar. Due to the warmth of the Paratha, sugar would melt and she would roll these pieces into small balls. Churi kay laddu requires a lot of patience and time management. If the Partha is too cold, we can never make churi kay laddu because the sugar will not melt or let flatbread pieces stick to one another.

Churi kay Laddu was the most favourite treat for children in Pakistan villages in old times when fancy ice cream, chocolate, and dessert was only a thing from imagination. Women would make churi kay laddu for children to make them happy.

My Nani had very soft hands. I still remember her, rolling flatbread pieces into small spheres, and handing them over to children. Sharing this recipe is like sharing a piece of my heart.

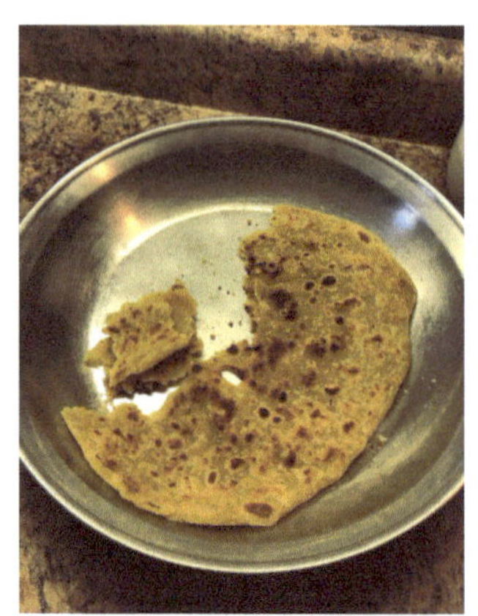

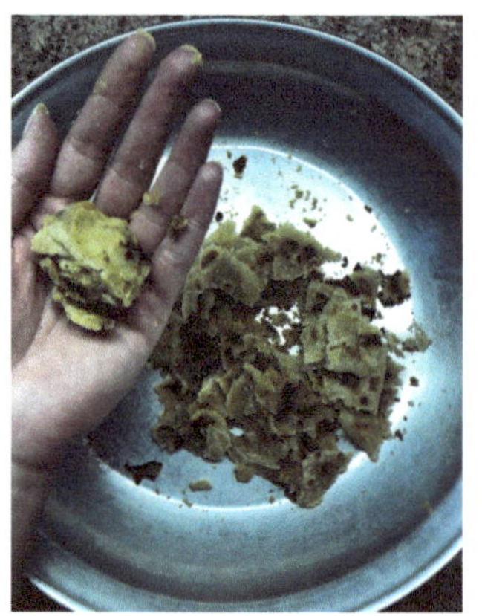

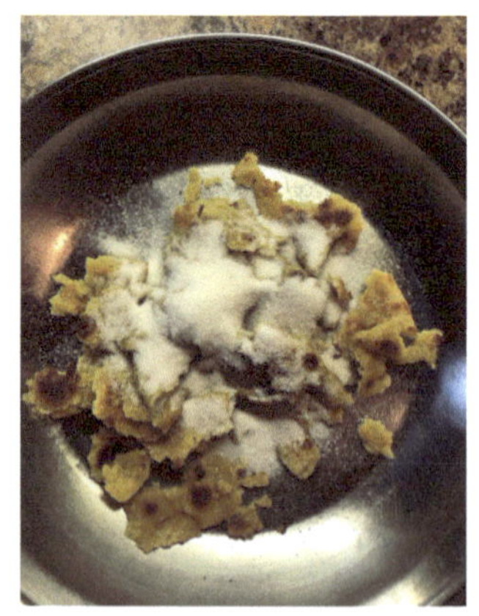

Churi Kay Laddu Recipe

Things we need:

2 cups wheat flour (Aata)

½ teaspoon salt

2 tablespoons sesi ghee

¾ cups water

5 tablespoons sugar

10 cups love

Paratha (flatbread):

Mix 2 tablespoons Desi ghee or 3 Tablespoons vegetable oil into the flour, mixing thoroughly into the dry flour before adding salt. Now, slowly start mixing the water into the flour. When the water is evenly combined with the flour and a mixture forms, make a fist and gently knead the mixture into a dough. Keep kneading while moistening hands with water. Add more water if needed. When a dough forms, let it sit for fifteen minutes before starting to make paratha.

After fifteen minutes, divide the dough into two parts. Make a ball (Pera) out of one half. Now sprinkle some dry flour on your clean kitchen counter, and with the help of a rolling pin, start flattening the dough into a large, flat circle.

Preheat a pan on medium heat and put the flattened circular dough in the pan. Let it cook until the dough starts changing colour and then flip. With the help of a tablespoon, add ghee or oil to one side of flatbread and flip. Add one tablespoon of ghee/oil to the other side and flip. Add Ghee/Oil only once on each side. Cook the paratha until golden brown and slightly crispy.

Dish out the paratha on a large plate and immediately break it into small pieces. Now, add five tablespoons of white or brown sugar to the paratha pieces. After thoroughly mixing sugar into a paratha, make small balls (Laddu) from that mixture. You can make them big or small, and make as many as you wish. I would make four out of one paratha. Don't forget to make paratha from the other half part of the dough.

Enjoy Churi kay Laddu!

Recipe

My recipe is a prayer

My kitchen is a temple

My house fills with aroma

My exhaust fan is the temple bell

That blasts that aroma into my neighborhood

Neighbors respond to that aroma and ask

"What are you cooking today?"

I say, "Nothing, but some offerings to make
my gods happy."

Haleem

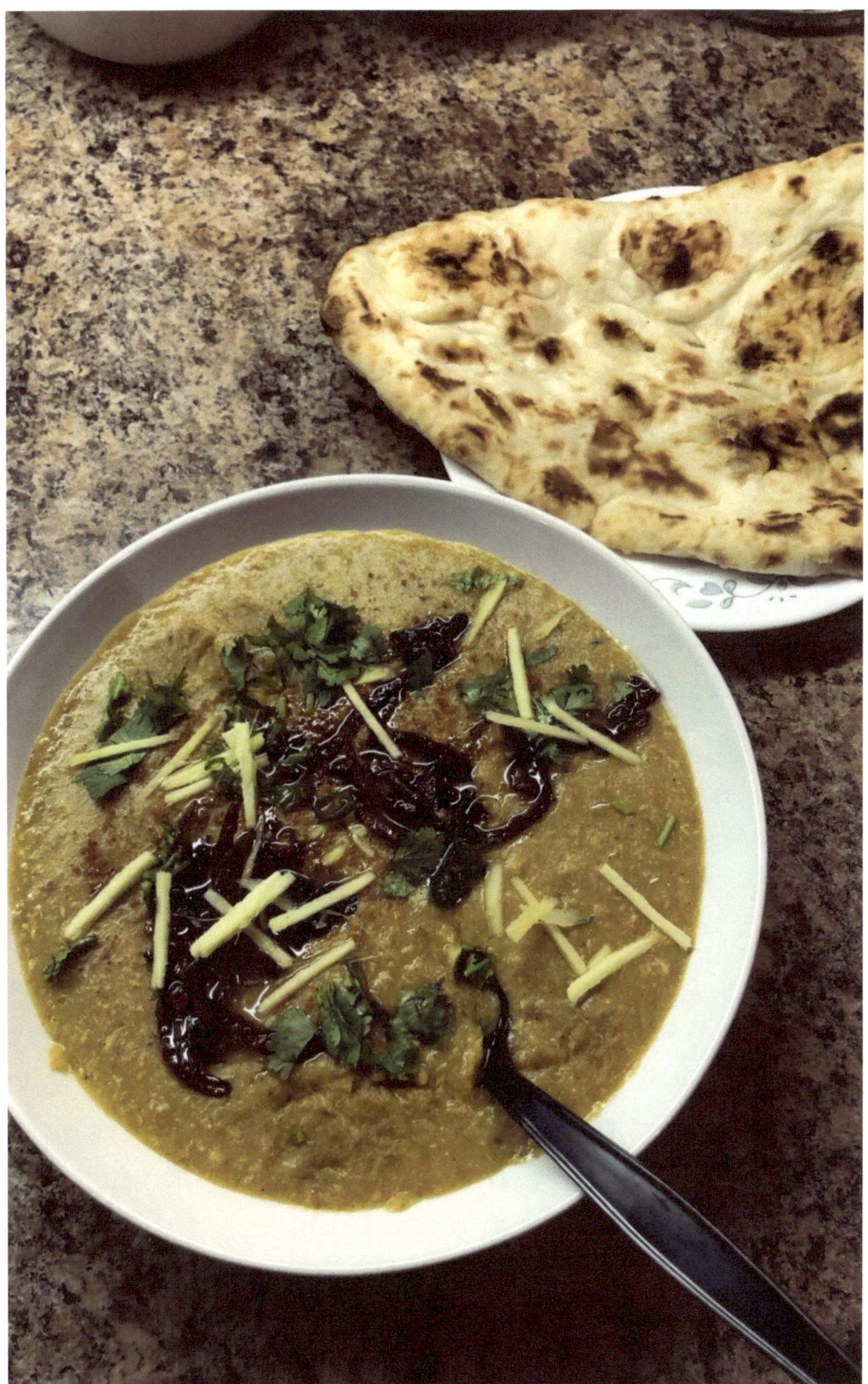

Nizams — who ruled over the state of Hyderabad, India, for two hundred and twenty-four years — originally belonged to the Asaf Jahi Turkic dynasty originating from Uzbekistan. Nizam ul Mulk was the title given to the seven Asaf Jah(s) who ruled over Hyderabad from 1724 to 1948. They initially came to India to serve the Mughal emperors. After the death of Aurangzaib, a Mughal Emperor, the Viceroy of Deccan — Asaf Jah 1 — declared independence and became the first Nizam of Hyderabad.

Nizams gradually became the wealthiest people in the world. They were very fond of food, literature, art, and architecture.

Shoaib Daniyal explains in his article "The History of Haleem" how the name Haleem comes from the Arabic dish Harees made with meat, wheat, cinnamon, and ghee. Shoaib narrates that Harees was brought to India by the Yemeni soldiers in Nizams' Army some ninety years ago.

Nizams who ruled over Hyderabad Deccan loved Yemeni loyalty and thus recruited soldiers from Yemen in their army and as their bodyguards. Yemeni soldiers used to cook Harees for themselves, but one of the subjects of Nizam introduced Harees to the Nizam as a part of their feast.

Nizam liked it so much, that it was later on permanently added to the menu served in Nizam's court.

Harees was very plain and lacked the savoury taste craved by the people of India. Indian spices and lentils (Daal) were added to the original recipe of Harees to make it taste more Indian. The improved dish was called "Haleem" rather than Harees. Later on, Haleem became one of the most popular dishes in India and Pakistan. Today, Bazaars in India and Pakistan have many Haleem selling shops which never go out of business.

Haleem Recipe

Ingredients

4 lbs. Boneless chicken or beef
1 ½ cup Oil
2 medium size onion sliced
2 tablespoons Red chili powder
2 tablespoons Turmeric powder
3 tablespoons Garlic paste
3 tablespoons Ginger paste
1 ½ cup Fried onion
2 cups Pot barley
2 cups Gayhoon (Wheat Barley)
1 cup Yellow Split Gram (Moong ki daal)
1 cup Red Lentil (Daal Masoor)
1 cup Black Gram Skinned (Uradh ki daal/Maash ki daal)
1 cup Bengal Gram Split (Chana ki daal)
1 cup Arhar ki daal (pigeon peas lentil)
1 cup Basmati rice
4 liters Water
1 ½ tablespoon Garam masala
(Refer to page 65 for Garam masala recipe)

Method

We cook meat and lentils separately and mix them later.

Part 1 (Preparing meat)

Fry sliced onion in 1 cup oil in a deep cooking pot for 8 to 9 minutes. Add meat and fry with onion for five minutes. Now add ginger and garlic paste and cook for ten minutes. Now add spices: salt, red chilli powder, turmeric powder and garam masala. Cook meat in spices for 10 minutes while adding little water. After frying meat in all the spices for five minutes, add 2 to 3 cups of water and cook until meat is tender. Beef usually takes hours to tenderize if you are not using instant pot; however, Chicken is ready in less time.

Part 2 (Cooking lentils)

Rinse and soak wheat barley, pot barley, yellow split gram lentil, red lentil, black gram skinned lentil, Bengal gram split lentil, arhar ki daal, and basmati rice in water for three hours before cooking.

After three hours, put everything together with 4 liters of water in a large cooking pot and boil for 4 to five hours or until tender. Keep stirring the pot from time to time. You can also use an instant pot to accelerate cooking. Change the amount of water needed to cook in an instant pot. Instant pots require less water. The amount of water in an instant pot depends on the size of instant pot.

Once all the lentils and rice are tender, mix cooked meat to the lentils, add 2 cups of water and cook for another 30 minutes. Keep stirring until everything is mixed evenly.

Top it with fried onion, mint, and Garam Masala, serve it with naan bread.

A Sweet Reminiscence

As soon as the eighth month of the Islamic calendar commences, a strange feeling engulfs my household. From food to social events, to religious significance, Shabaan is a month close to our hearts. When I came to Canada in 2005, I completely lost the sense of celebration. As I was away from home, it was not easy to indulge in the spirit of celebration.

Shabaan is a month filled with innumerable childhood memories. The fourteenth night of Shabaan is called as Shab-e-Baraat — the night of forgiveness in Arabic. It is a big night which is celebrated by rich and poor alike in Pakistan. People make sweets of various kinds, share them with neighbours, and stay up all night in prayers till dawn. For Shab - e - Baraat, my family makes sweet tarts (Meethi Tikiya) from semolina and white flour mixed with cardamom, nuts, oil, and sugar. Making Meethi Tikiya on Shab - e - Baraat is not only a tradition passed on from one generation to another, but it is also the most cherished memory of my childhood.

I imagine myself standing where I saw my daughter this year — cutting circles in flattened dough with a glass before throwing each Tikiya in the oil for deep frying.

During the lockdown, I tried to teach my daughters some family traditions. As I was teaching them the art of mixing the right amount of semolina and flour necessary to make Tikiya dough, my mind pulled me back into the nineties.

I pictured myself sitting on a Peeri (a low sitting chair) beside the stove running on gas cylinders, a deep-frying pan on the stove, inundated with oil, waiting to turn the dough into the most delicious and crispiest brown Tikiya.

Methane was not readily available in those times. One had to fill the cylinder at a station and bring it home before anyone could cook. We would wait for Ammi (Mom) to finish kneading before we could finally make the perfect circles in the flattened dough with glass. The final part was always beautiful, night culminating with Nazar (a little prayer), candles lit all over the place while we finally sat and ate.

A part of all the festivities owas Charaghaan (lighting of candles) on rooftops and fireworks on the fourteenth night. We don't do fireworks here in Canada, but light candles and pray for health and peace; especially for the people living in war zones.

I could see all that in my daughters now: the excitement, the struggle, the wait. I am content that I have given my children what my mother had passed on to me.

Meethi Tikiya

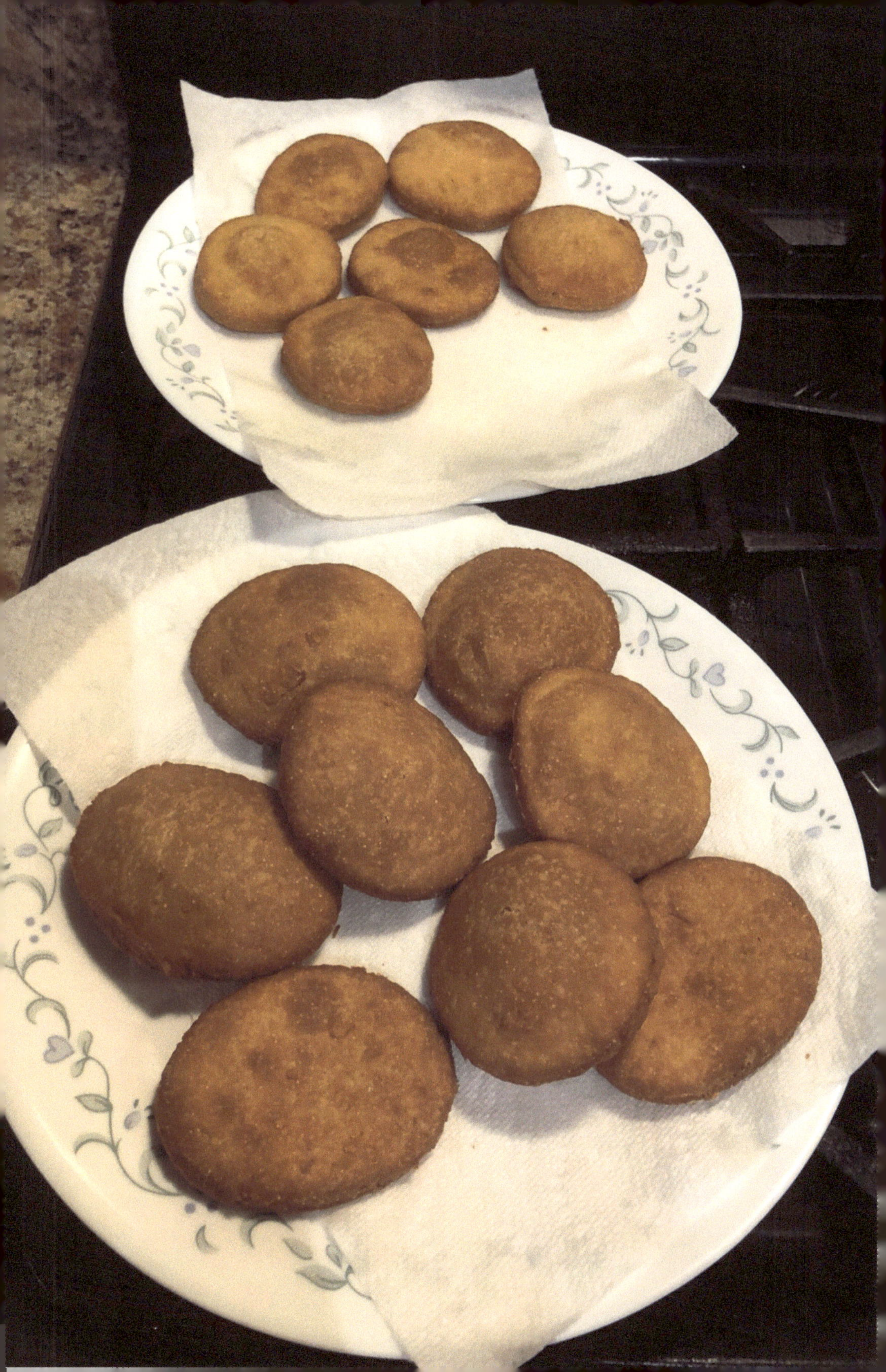

Meethi Tikiya Recipe

2 cups all-purpose flour

¼ cup semolina

1/4 cup ghee 1/4 cup

3/4 cups sugar

8 crushed cardamoms

2/3 cups water

Method

Mix all ingredients into a dough and let it sit for an hour. Cover it with a lid. After an hour, flatten the dough with the help of a rolling pin and use a cookie cutter to cut out circles.
Preheat vegetable oil in a large pan on medium heat. Carefully slide in the cut-out circles. Let the Tikiya fry until it turns golden. Keep flipping the Tikiya from time to time with a spatula. Take out the Tikiya when Golden brown.

Maash Ki Daal
Black Gram Lentil

Maash ki daal (Black Gram Lentil)

Ingredients

2 cups maash ki daal (split and skinned black gram lentil)

2 tablespoons ginger (crushed)

1 ½ teaspoon salt

1 ½ teaspoon crushed red chili flakes

4 cups water

1 medium size onion

Mint for garnish

Method:

Wash raw lentils with tap water 3 to 4 times.
After washing the lentil, put it in a pot and add 3 cups of water. Boil the lentil after adding salt, crushed red chilli pepper, crushed ginger. When the Lentil starts boiling, lower the flame and let it cook for 30 minutes or until water starts drying up and daal (Lentil) becomes soft and tender.
Turn the stove off and now prepare the garnish. Maash lentil is usually garnished with baghaar (see recipe below).

Baghaar (garnish) preparation

Take 1 medium size onion, cut it into thin slices. Fry the onion slices in oil until it becomes crisp and blackish-brown in colour. Now pour the onion along with the oil on top of the cooked lentil. You can also sprinkle some chopped mint on top.

Enjoy with naan, roti, flatbread, or pita bread!

Arraying into Mughal designs

Pakistan is a land which is rich in cultural heritage. It was a part of India before the partition in 1947. Mughals reigned over this land for over 300 years before the British Crown took over in 1858 and ruled for a century.

Hundred years do not sound a lot but are enough to colonize a region. Food, traditions, clothes, and lifestyle in Pakistan echo with remnants of the glorious Mughal era and a few strains of British Raj visibly alive in the lifestyle of aristocrats.

Mughal emperors had a luxurious lifestyle; they ate in gold and silver dishes and wore silks. Finest local artists and tailors would make the clothes worn by the emperors. Prints and textures from the Mughal archives and paintings still inspire present-day Pakistani dresses. Rich colours, textures, geometrical shapes, and calligraphy designs used in printmaking today help one retrospect the dresses worn in those times.

Quite interestingly, these prints were worn by men rather than women in the Mughal era, but today it is the opposite and we find the patterns mostly in women's clothing. You will find arches, floral designs, textures, and geometrical shapes in Pakistani dresses.

Trained artists and experts spend hours creating eye-catching designs and prints. Extremely talented tailors then transform the fabric into traditional Pakistani dresses.

The market for these dresses is expanding as the demand for Pakistani clothes by ex-pat Pakistani women and western women is increasing.

Ten years ago, ordering Pakistani dresses from Canada was not easy, but now Pakistani designers have websites where I can select designs, fabrics, and colours with great ease.

Here are some of the prints from my Pakistani dresses.

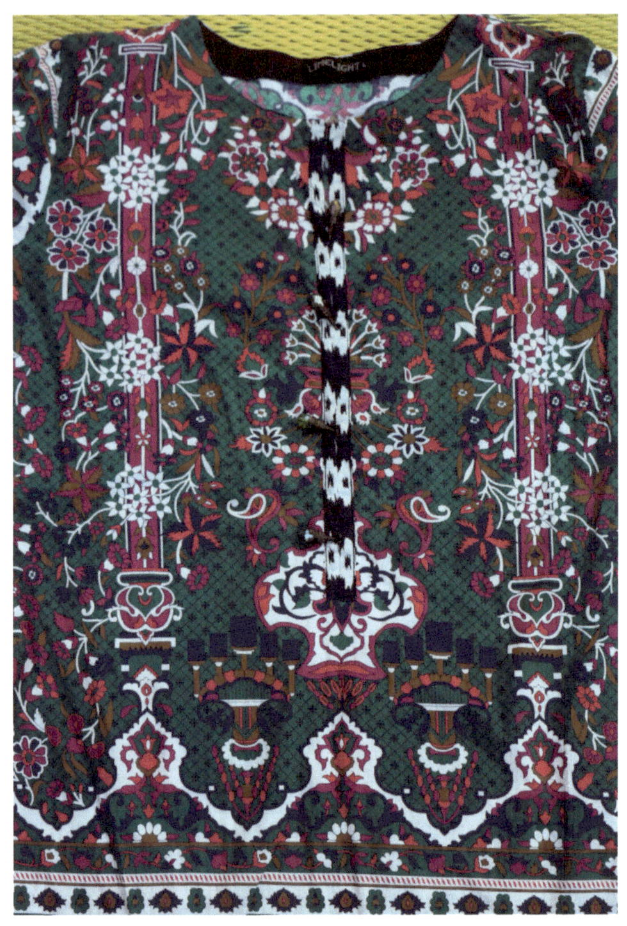

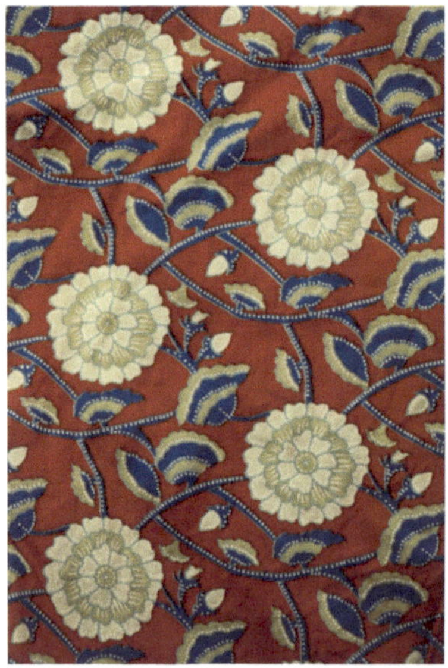

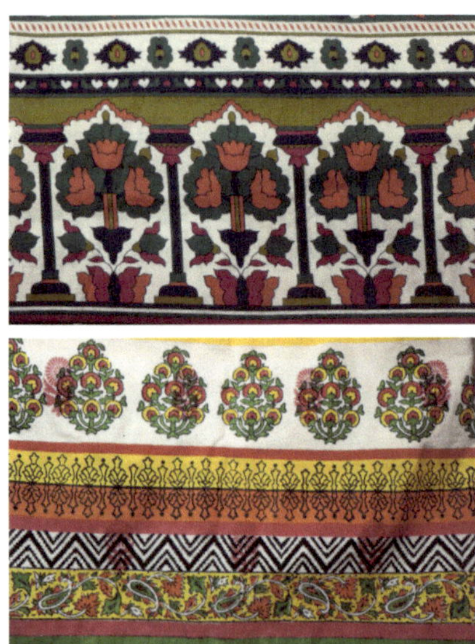

Translating Shah Hussain's Kafi

Sufism (Mysticism) does not portray Islam's real spirit say some religious pundits. However, Sufism is the spiritual realm in which Muslims look for paths that connects them with the omnipotent and find ways to acquire closeness to the one who rules the universe. Sufis first learn through their spiritual journey under the guidance of their teachers and then teach it to others through their poetry and discourse. Among many Muslim Sufi poets, Shah Hussain holds a very elevated stature and is one of my favorites. He was a Punjabi Sufi Poet who lived in the 16 century and is known as the pioneer of Kafi. Kafi is one of the genres of Punjabi Sufi Poetry.

Shah Hussain fell in love with Madhu Lal — a Hindu boy with the most enchanting beauty. Legend says that Shah Hussain circumambulated Madho's home for many years until he embraced Islam and Shah Hussain became his spiritual teacher. Later Shah Hussain renamed himself as Madho Lal Hussain and believed that Madho Lal and Shah Hussain were one entity.

While I was reading about Madho Lal Hussain, I learned that there are two graves in his shrine at Baghbanpura, Lahore where Sheikh Madhu and Lal Hussain (Shah Hussain) are resting side by side.

I have written poetic translations of a couple of his Kafis. This one is about a girl longing for her beloved while he lives far away in another country. On the other hand, this can also be interpreted as an ascetic's longing to see his Creator.

Men Wi Jhok Ranjhan Di Janran

Main Wi Jhok Ranjhan Di Janran
Naal Meray Koi Challay

I too have to go
To the land of my beloved
Is there anyone who can accompany?

Pairie Poundi, Mintaan Kardi
Janran Taan Piya Akallay

I have implored each person known
Yet I embark on the journey alone

Nain Wi Dungi, Tilla Puraraan
Sheehaan Pattanr Mallay

The river is deep and the bridge is old
The boat shudders when the lions roar

Jera Mittraan Di Khabar Lay Aaway
Main Hath Day Deniyyan Challay

To him, I relinquish all my jewels
Whoever brings my Amy's news

Ratain Dard Deehaan Darmandi
Ghaao Mitraan Day Alheh

Nights are misery, days are worn
My heart is bleeding, my body's torn

Ranjharn Yaar Tabeeb Suneenda
Main Tan Dard Awallay

My beloved's famous for his miracle cure
Take me to him I can wait no more

Kahay Hussain Faqeer Nimanaan
Saayeen Suneenray Ghallay

Oh lord! Says Husain "I can't endure;
Summon me to the heaven's door"

Palak Aaloo Curry

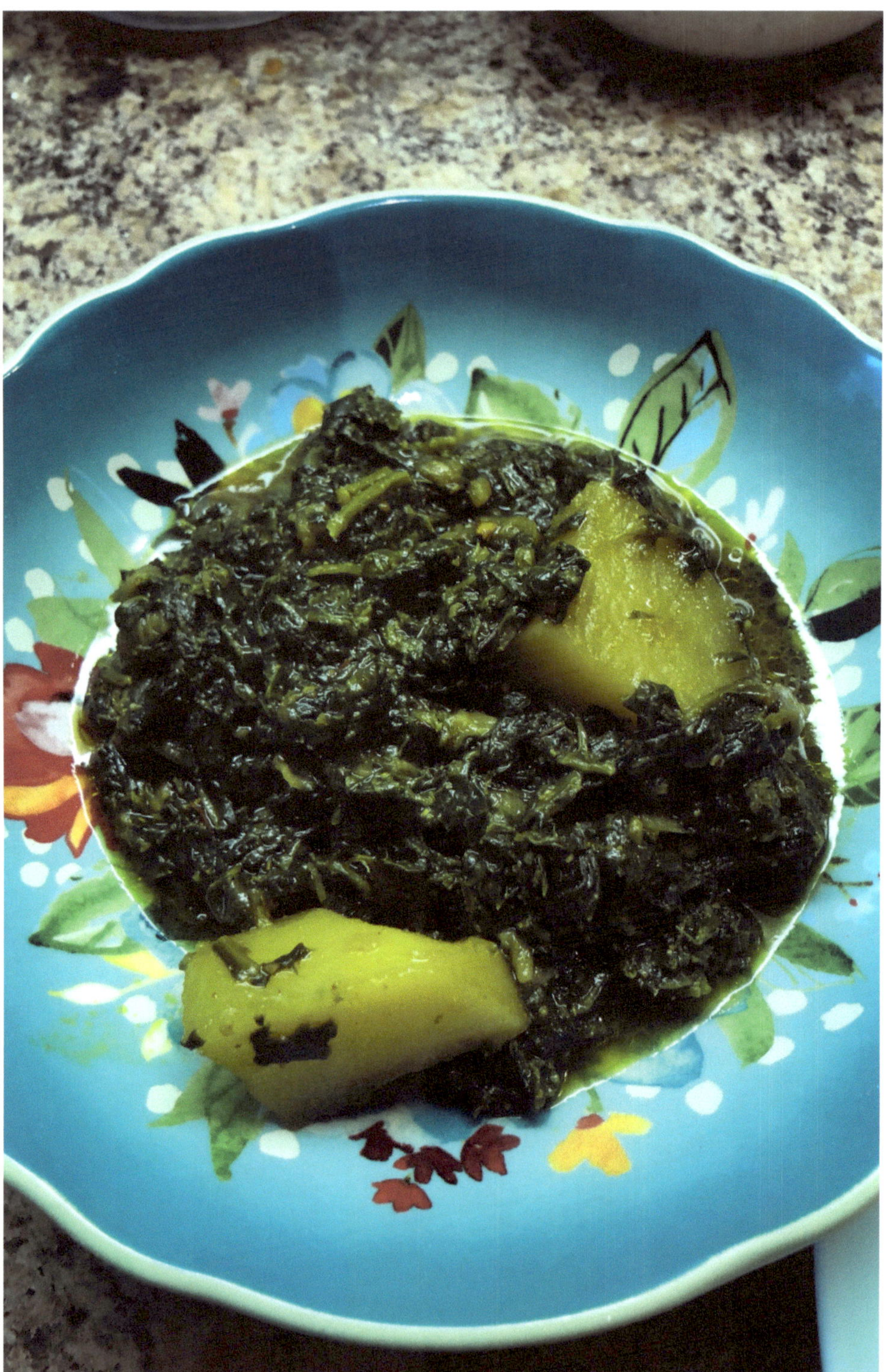

Palak Aaloo (Spinach and Potato) Curry Recipe

Ingredients:

624 grams Spinach

2 medium size potatoes cut into cubes

3 ½ teaspoons coriander seeds crushed powder

1 ½ teaspoon turmeric powder

1 ½ teaspoon salt

1 teaspoon cumin seeds

1 teaspoon mustard seeds (Rai dana)

½ teaspoon Fenugreek (Methi dana)

2 teaspoons red chili powder

½ teaspoon red chili flakes

8 tablespoons oil

1 tablespoon garlic paste

1 tablespoon crushed ginger

3 medium sliced onion

Preparation:

Cut onion into slices, preheat vegetable oil in a cooking pot, and add sliced onions. When the onion start turning brown, add cumin seeds, mustard seeds. Fenugreek, and let them fry with onion. After 3 to 4 minutes, add ginger and garlic paste. Let all the ingredients fry for another 4 minutes, then add 1/2 a cup of water, salt, red chilli powder, red chilli flakes, crushed coriander seeds (powder), and turmeric powder to the onion. Cook for another 5 minutes; keep stirring. Now add potatoes and fry them in the spices for 5 to 10 minutes. Keep adding water little by little, and stir. When the potatoes change their colour, add Spinach and stir. Mix the Spinach well with the potatoes, spices and cook for another 5 to 10 minutes. Now add 1 cup of water and cook on medium to low heat while covered. Let it cook for 20 to 25 minutes or until potatoes are tender and Spinach changes to dark green colour. Enjoy it with chapatti bread, naan bread, or rice.

Naan Bread

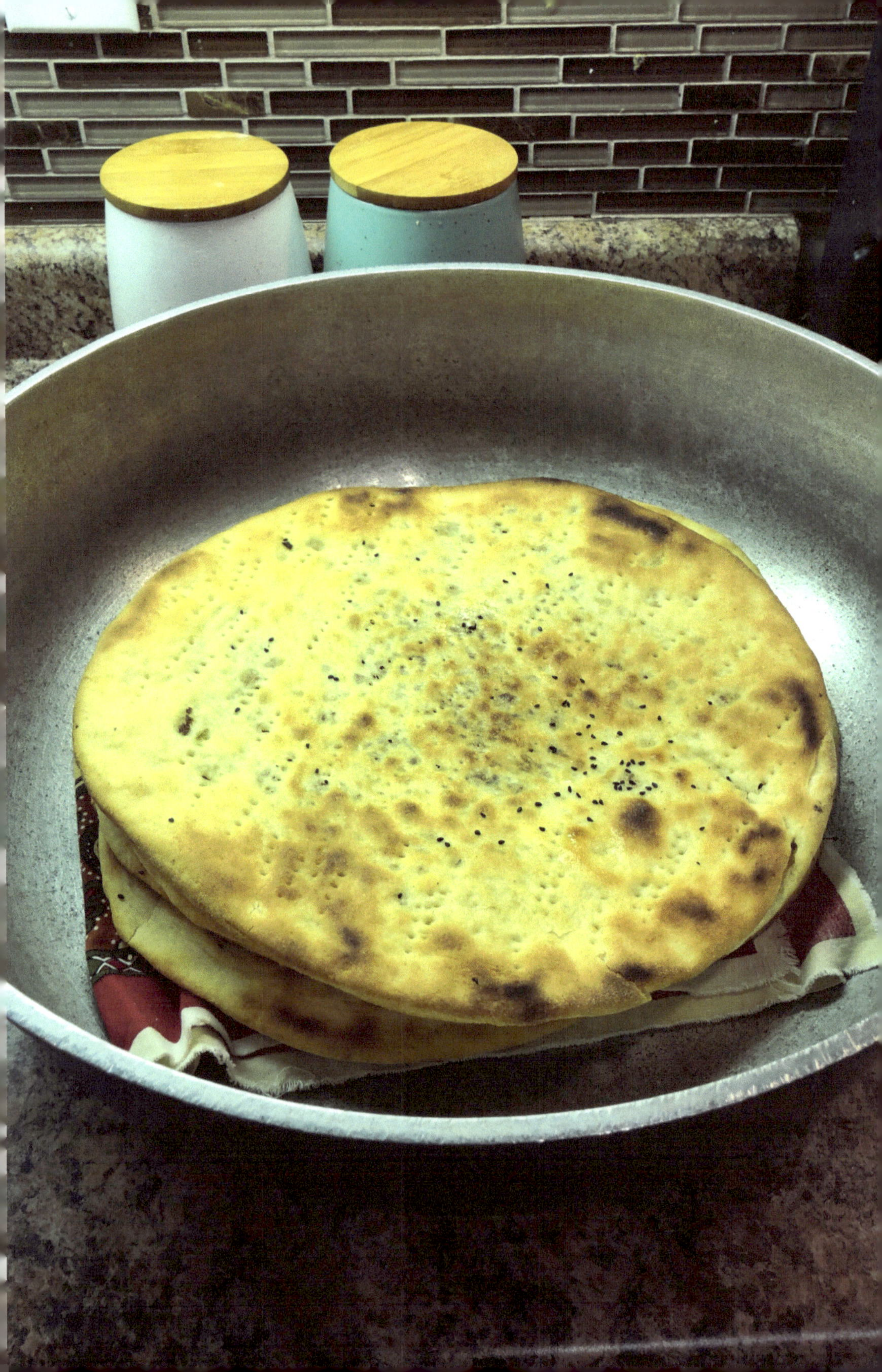

Naan Bread Recipe

Ingredients

3 ½ cups all-purpose flour
1 ½ tablespoon quick rise yeast
2 cups water
4 tablespoons oil
1 teaspoon salt
1 teaspoon sugar

Method:

Mix yeast and sugar in 1 cup of warm water and set aside to rise (5 to 8 minutes). Add salt and oil to all-purpose flour and spread it evenly with your hands. Now add yeast water to the flour and mix well. Gradually add one more cup of water while mixing. It won't look like a dough, but a rough mixture. Cover this mixture with a piece of cloth and put it in a corner for 40 minutes to rise.

After 40 minutes, knead the dough, cover it again and set it aside for another 30. After 30 minutes, knead the dough again and divide it into 3 small balls or 2 big balls.

Preheat oven to 500 °F. Gently flatten the dough balls and make medium size circles like tortillas. Brush a round pizza tray with oil and spread the flattened dough on it. Poke the flattened dough with a fork randomly to create some textures.

Once done, throw the tray into the oven and let the dough cook until bubbles start rising and the colour of naan becomes golden brown. If you like, you can take the tray out in the middle of baking and flip half-cooked naan to cook both sides evenly. Once the naan is golden brown, take it out and brush it with oil lightly. Keep the naan in a cloth and put it inside a pot; otherwise, naan will get cold and hard. Keep them inside the box until served.

Enjoy!

TIP: Softer the dough, softer the naan.

Bihari Kababs

Bihar is a province in East India which is famous for many things, notably its wise people and delicious food. Legend has it that the people of Bihar are born with remarkable skills and unparalleled wisdom. Among the food, there is a list of dishes which are loved all over the world, but the most favourite one is Bihari Kababs. This dish is very famous in Pakistan, India, and the rest of the world wherever the people of Bihar migrated. They took their famous recipe with them and everywhere it became the talk of the town. I tasted it first time in Canada, and I learned this recipe from my sister-in-law.

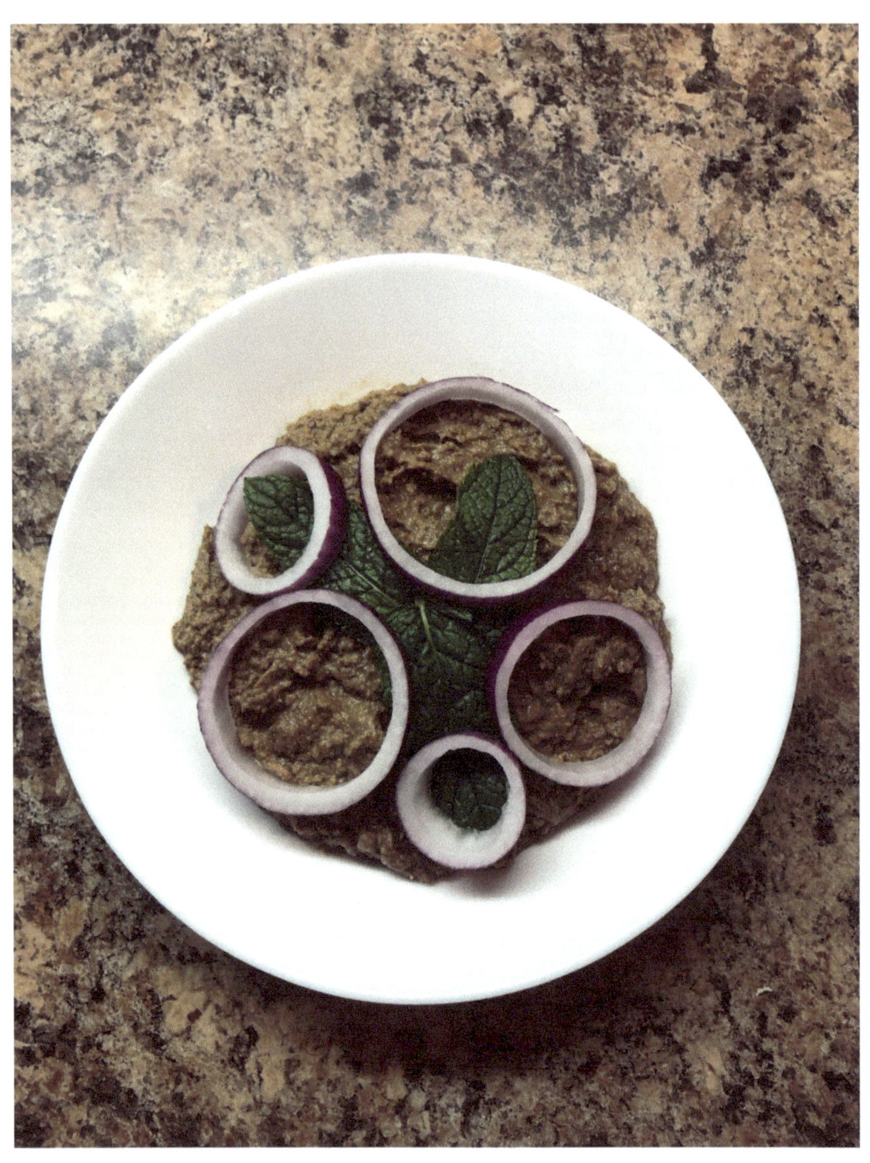

Bihari Kabab recipe

2 lbs minced beef (qeema)

3 tablespoon zeera (roasted crushed cumin seeds)

2 teaspoon black pepper crushed

5 teaspoons red chili powder

2 teaspoon garam masala
(Refer to garam masala recipe on page 54)

1 tablespoon ginger paste

1 cup oil

4 tablespoons fried onion

4 tablespoons bhuna hua besan (roasted chickpea flour)

2 teaspoon salt

6 tablespoons crushed papaya

Procedure

Grind papaya and ginger to make a paste. Mix everything and marinate the mixture for about 5 hours. After 5 hours, heat oil and put marinated mixture in it while stirring. Fry the kababs for 10 minutes then add 1 ½ cup of water and cook until it turns brown (approximately 45 to 60 minutes). Top it with raw onion rings and mint leaves.

Karahi Chicken Curry Recipe

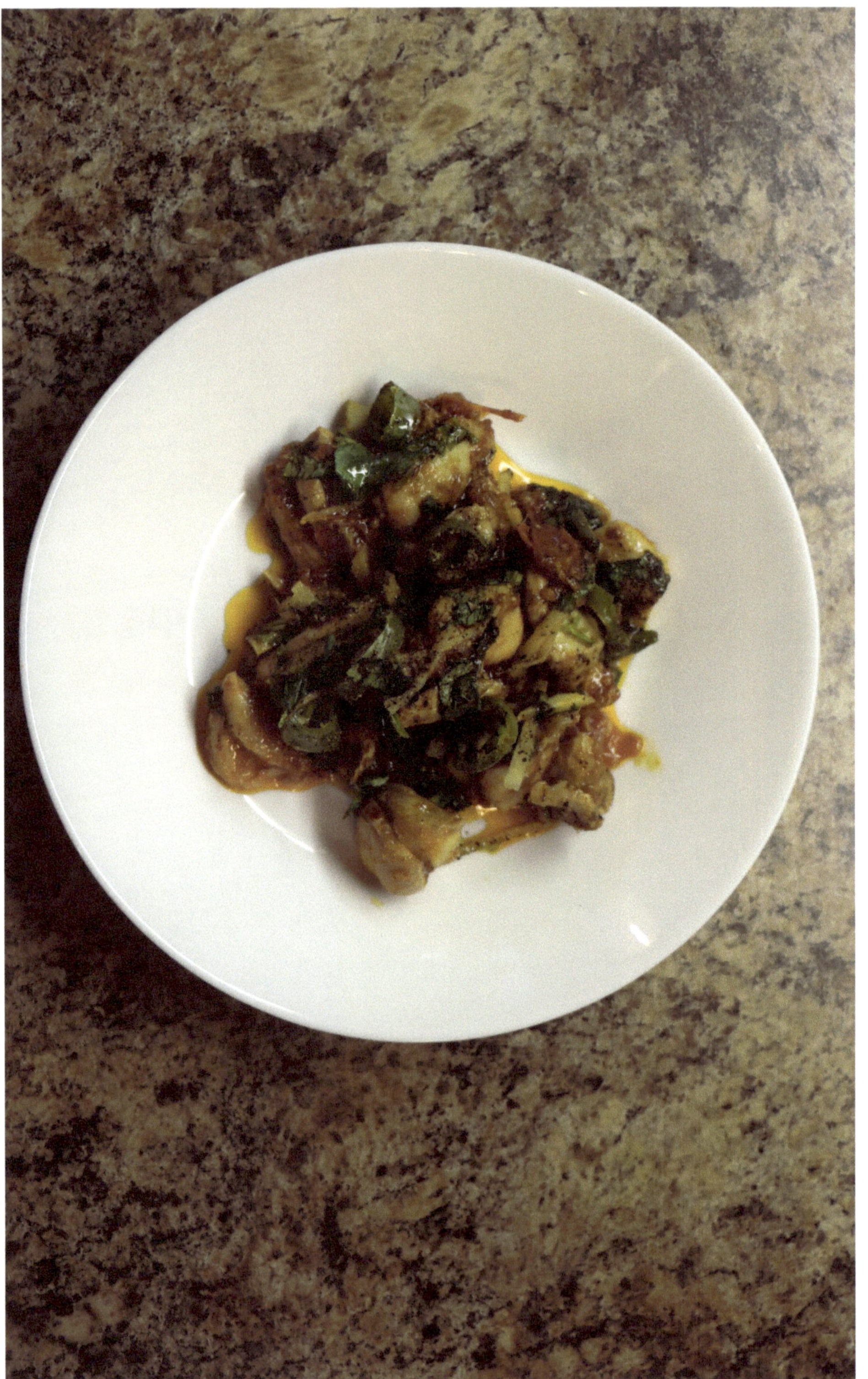

Karahi Chicken Curry recipe

2 lbs. boneless chicken
6 to 8 tablespoons oil
1 tablespoon garlic paste
1 tablespoon ginger paste
1 teaspoon black pepper
1 teaspoon red chili powder
1 and ½ teaspoon salt
1 ½ teaspoon roasted cumin power
1 cup water
4 medium-sized tomatoes cut into cubes
2 to 3 chopped green chilies
cilantro for garnish

Procedure

Preheat oil in a deep cooking pan, add chicken and let it fry for 5 minutes or until it changes colour. Now add ginger and garlic paste. Let the chicken cook in ginger and garlic paste for about ten minutes. After 10 minutes, add tomatoes and cook for about fifteen minutes or until tomatoes changes into a paste. Now add salt, red chilli powder and roaster cumin powder. Cook the entire mixture for about ten minutes. Now add 1 cup water, cover and cook for another twenty minutes.

Finally, add green chilies, sprinkle the curry with black pepper and garnish with cilantro. Eat with plain white rice, Naan bread, and flatbread.

Garam Masala

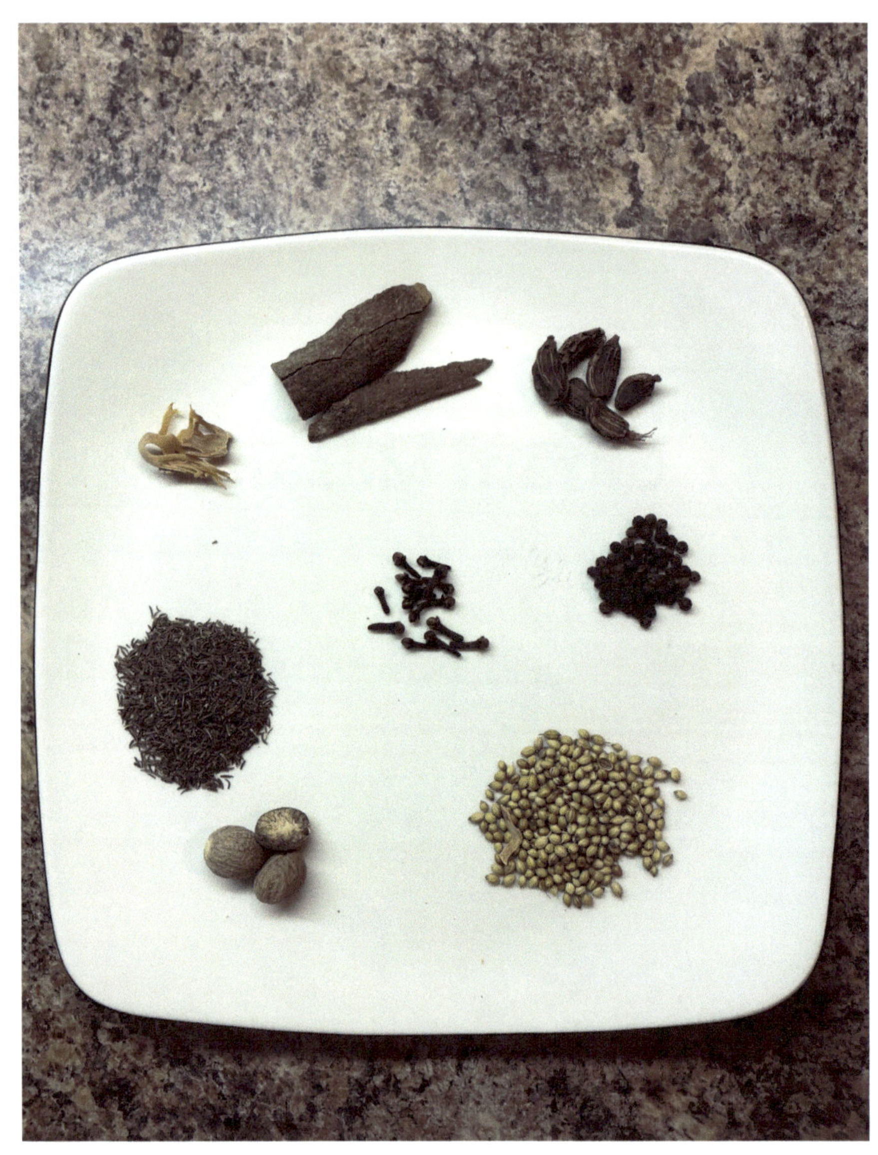

Garam Masala

Ingredients:

1 table spoon ground big black cardamom

1 tablespoon ground black cumin seeds

1 tablespoon ground black pepper

1 tablespoon ground nutmeg

1 table spoon ground cloves

1 table spoon ground cinnamon sticks

1 table spoon ground coriander seeds

Preparation:

Mix all of these ingredients together and there you have the authentic Garam Masala.

Seekh kababs

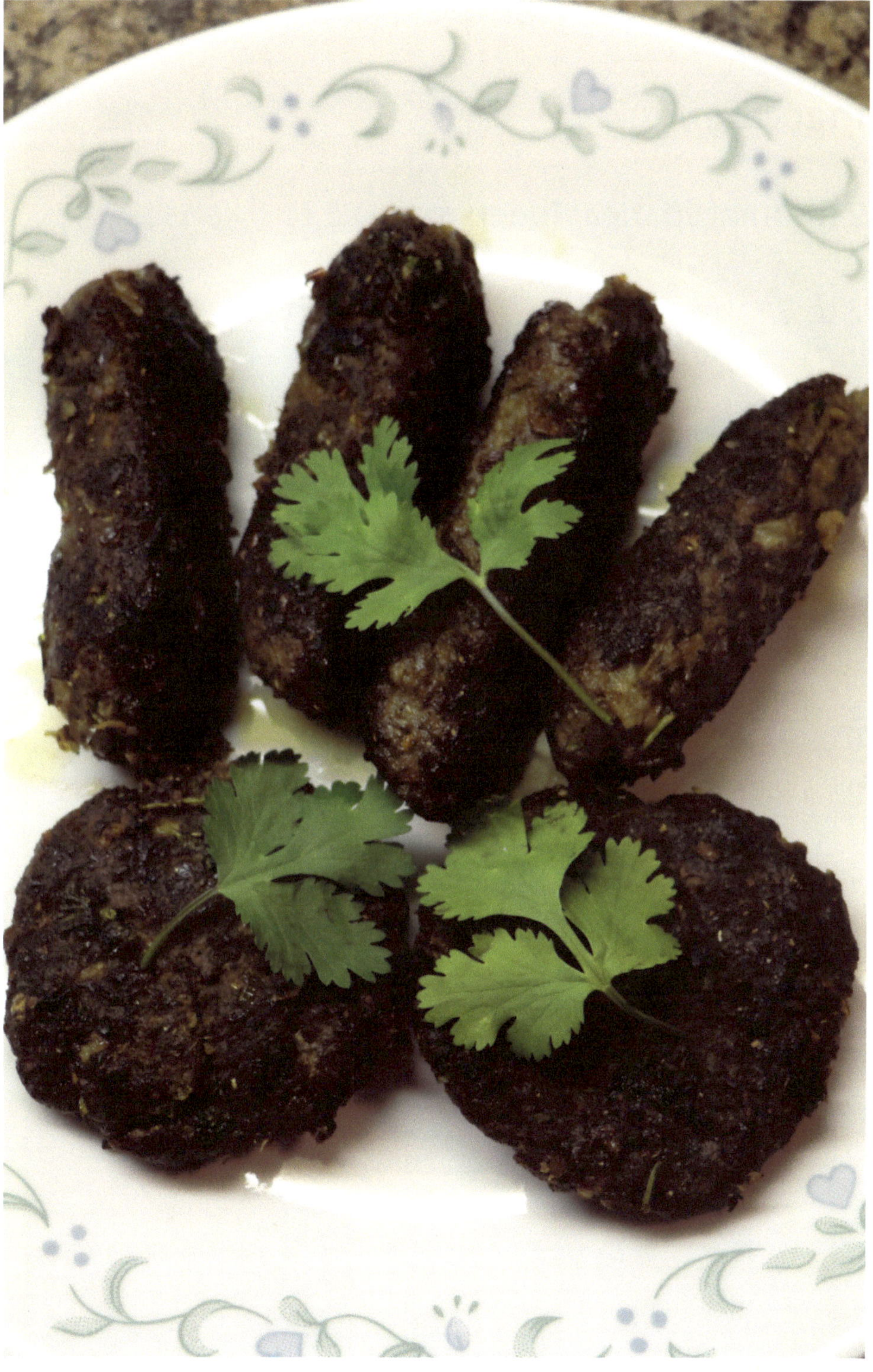

Seekh Kabab Recipe

Ingredients:

2 lbs minced meat (beef) makes 5 to 6 kababs

7 to 8 tablespoons oil for shallow frying

1 ½ teaspoon salt 1 ½ teaspoon

2 ½ teaspoon roasted and crushed coriander seeds

Fennel seed crushed powder 2 ½ teaspoon

Crushed red chili pepper 1 teaspoon

2 to 3 small chopped green chilies

1 teaspoon garam masala

3 tablespoons crushed fried onion

1 small fresh onion crushed

6 pieces crushed garlic

2 tablespoon ginger

3 tablespoon fresh coriander chopped

Method:

Mix all the ingredients thoroughly in a bowl and set aside for 1 hour. After one hour, mix the ingredients one more time by hand.
Preheat oil in a pan, make patties or long kababs on a skewer from the mixture according to your choice. Carefully put the kababs in the pan and shallow fry on medium heat until dark brown. Keep flipping the kababs every 2 minutes while frying. If using an air fryer, flip the Kababs once.

Enjoy them in a bun, with flatbread, rice, or just as is.

Work Citations

Shoaib Danial, "The history of haleem: How a bland iftar dish from Yemen got Indianised" *The Sunday Guardian*, 2014. 978-1-7780332-0-9 (Page 31)

Trans. N. Husayn Mardi, "Various Sayings of Imam 'Ali Ibn Abi Talib, An Extract of Du'a Kumayl", *Chehel Sotoon Theological School*: Iran, 1989. 978-1-7780332-0-9 (Page 1a)

Schimmel, A.. "Sufism." *Encyclopedia Britannica*, November 20, 2019. 978-1-7780332-0-9 (Page 57) https://www.britannica.com/topic/Sufism.

About The Author

Seemab Zahra is a multidisciplinary artist in Waterloo, Canada. She was born in the Punjab province of Pakistan — a region famous for its vast green fields, singing rivers, Sufi poets, and ancient folklore. In 2005, Seemab moved to Canada, and since then she has lived in three different cities: Toronto, Cambridge, and Kitchener.

Seemab expresses herself through her poetry, photography, and writing. Her work gives the reader a sense of her connection with people and places she longs to see. Seemab shares her views on women's rights, Islamophobia, human rights, culture, and history. Her articles and photography have been published in various magazines in Canada and Pakistan, and India.

Besides poetry, writing, and photography, Seemab spends time cooking and sharing her family recipes through her Instagram.

She wrote this book to preserve her family recipes, share her connection with her history and leave behind a legacy for future generations.

At the 100 Notebook project public display

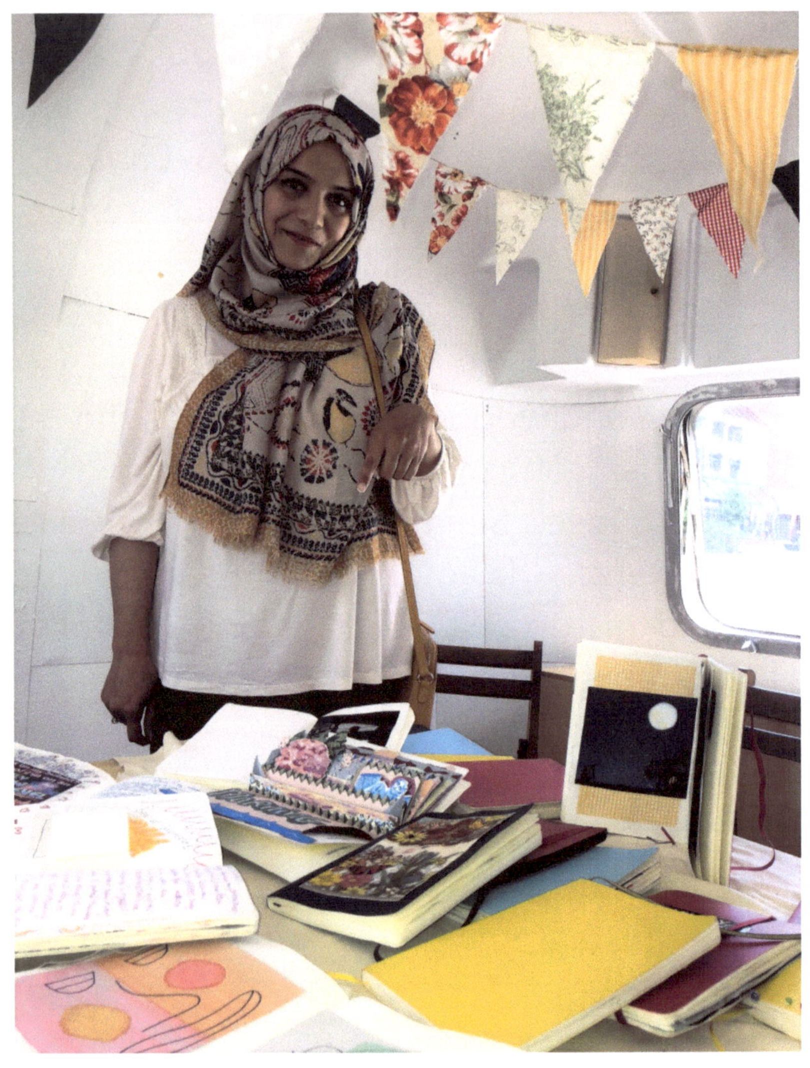

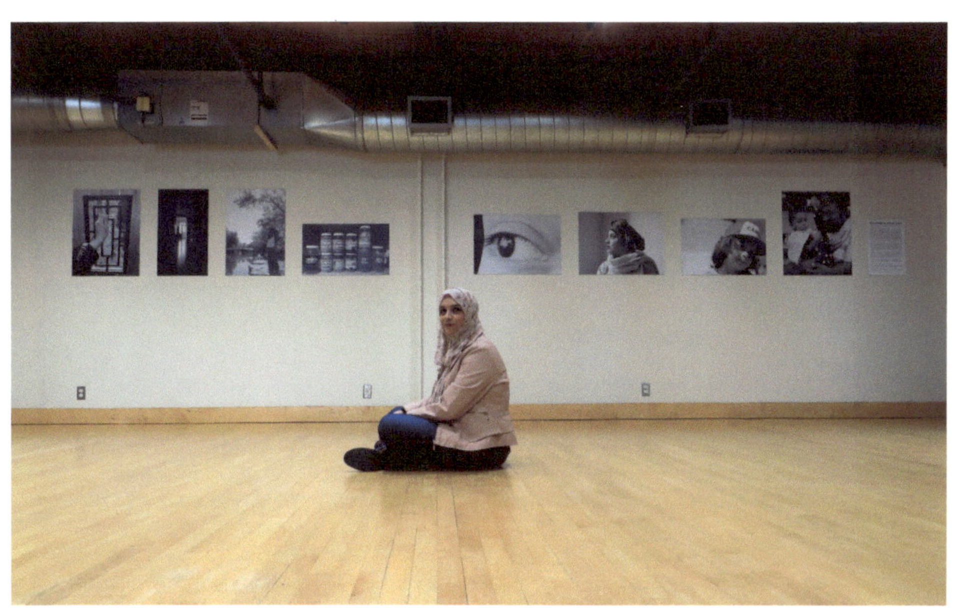

Photography Exhibition
at THEMUSEUM

Dec 2020 - May 2021

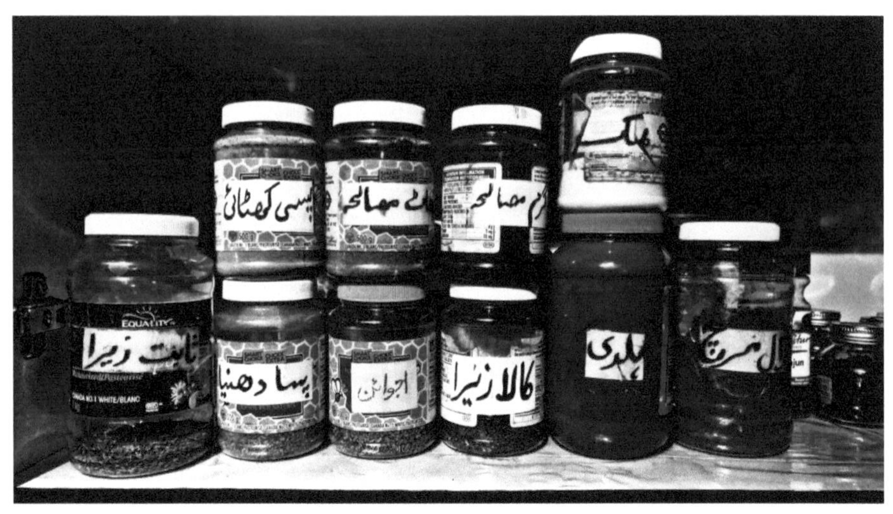

Spices from my pantry

One of the photos from my exhibition at THEMUSEUM Kitchener